40p

You've Come a Long Way, Snoopy

Charles M. Schulz

Selected cartoons from
THOMPSON IS IN TROUBLE,
CHARLIE BROWN, VOL. 1

D1440244

CORONET BOOKS
Hodder Fawcett, London

Copyright © 1972, 1973 by United Feature Syndicate, Inc.

First published 1976 by Fawcett Publications, Inc.,
New York

Coronet edition 1977
Third impression 1978

Printed in Great Britain for Hodder
Fawcett Ltd., Mill Road, Dunton Green,
Sevenoaks, Kent (Editorial Office: 47
Bedford Square, London, WC1 3DP) by
C. Nicholls & Company Ltd
The Philips Park Press, Manchester

ISBN 0 340 22159 3

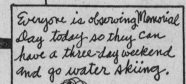

AT FIRST, I WANTED TO BE AN ONLY CHILD

YOU SPOILED THAT! THEN I THOUGHT MAYBE IT WOULD BE KIND OF NICE TO HAVE A SISTER.. SO WHAT HAPPENS? I GET ANOTHER BROTHER.. A RERUN!

THAT'S IT!

WE'LL CALL HIM "RERUN"!

"RERUN" VAN PELT... GOOD GRIEF!

"HUNDREDS OF PIRATES SWARMED ABOARD THE SHIP"

"THE CABIN BOY WAS WOUNDED SO HE PLAYED POSSUM"

WHEN A PERSON PRETENDS THAT HE'S DEAD, WE CALL IT "PLAYING POSSUM"

WHAT DO THE POSSUMS CALL IT?

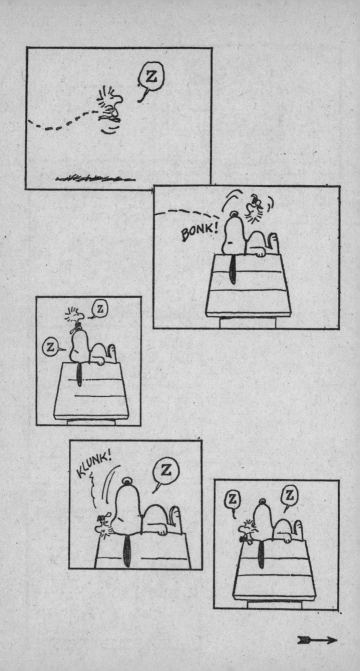

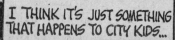

ARE WE GOING AROUND THE LAKE THIS YEAR, AND VISIT THE BOYS' CAMP, SIR?

I DON'T KNOW...MAYBE WE SHOULD JUST STAY HERE, AND SEE IF THEY VISIT US...

IT'S A LONG DAY, AND IT'S A BIG LAKE..

AND LIFE IS TOO SHORT... LET'S GO!!

I LIKE YOUR WAY OF THINKING, SIR!

STOP CALLING ME "SIR"!

I STOOD IN FRONT OF THAT LITTLE RED-HAIRED GIRL AND I SAW HOW PRETTY SHE WAS...

SUDDENLY, I REALIZED WHY CHUCK HAS ALWAYS LOVED HER, AND I REALIZED THAT NO ONE WOULD EVER LOVE ME THAT WAY..

I STARTED TO CRY, AND I COULDN'T STOP...I MADE A FOOL OUT OF MYSELF, BUT I DIDN'T CARE! I JUST LOOKED AT HER AND I CRIED AND CRIED AND CRIED...

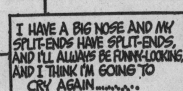

I HAVE A BIG NOSE AND MY SPLIT-ENDS HAVE SPLIT-ENDS, AND I'LL ALWAYS BE FUNNY-LOOKING, AND I THINK I'M GOING TO CRY AGAIN............

I LOOKED AT THAT LITTLE RED HAIRED GIRL, LINUS, AND I STARTED TO CRY AND I COULDN'T STOP..

SHE'S SO PRETTY..SHE JUST SORT OF SPARKLES..I'LL NEVER SPARKLE..I'M A MUD FENCE..I'M A PLAIN JANE...I FEEL LIKE THE GIRL WHO WANTED TO GO INTO THE BACK YARD AND EAT WORMS...

THE ONLY PERSON WHO EVER KNOWS HOW I FEEL IS SNOOPY.. IF SNOOPY WERE HERE, HE'D LEAN OVER AND KISS ME ON THE CHEEK..

♡ SMAK! ♡

LIKE THIS, SWEETIE?

Now is the time for all foxes to jump over the lazy dog.

SOMEHOW, THAT DOESN'T SEEM QUITE RIGHT...

WHAT A GREAT TITLE FOR MY NEW BOOK...

"THINGS I'VE LEARNED AFTER IT WAS TOO LATE"

Things I've Learned After It Was Too late.

A whole stack of memories will never equal one little hope.

I KIND OF LIKE THAT

WELL, HOW DO YOU LIKE HAVING A NEW BABY BROTHER?

OH, "RERUN" IS ALL RIGHT, I GUESS...ACTUALLY, I'D ALWAYS HOPED TO BE AN ONLY CHILD, BUT IT'S TOO LATE FOR THAT NOW...

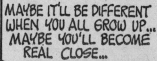

MAYBE IT'LL BE DIFFERENT WHEN YOU ALL GROW UP... MAYBE YOU'LL BECOME REAL CLOSE...

JOE FAMILY!

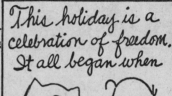

I'LL NEVER BE A BIG-LEAGUE PLAYER! I JUST DON'T HAVE IT! ALL MY LIFE I'VE DREAMED OF PLAYING IN THE BIG LEAGUES, BUT I KNOW I'LL NEVER MAKE IT...

YOU'RE THINKING TOO FAR AHEAD, CHARLIE BROWN...WHAT YOU NEED TO DO IS TO SET YOURSELF MORE IMMEDIATE GOALS...

IMMEDIATE GOALS?

YES

START WITH THIS NEXT INNING WHEN YOU GO OUT TO PITCH..

SEE IF YOU CAN WALK OUT TO THE MOUND WITHOUT FALLING DOWN!

THIS IS THE KIND OF EVENING THAT BRINGS BACK MEMORIES OF THE DAISY HILL PUPPY FARM

AFTER SUPPER, A COUPLE OF OTHER DOGS AND I USED TO CHASE EACH OTHER AROUND THE YARD...IT WAS A GOOD GAME..

THE RULES WERE SIMPLE

WOODSTOCK SAYS THERE'S A STRANGE CREATURE IN HIS NEST..

I'LL BET I COULD CLIMB THAT TREE IF SOMEONE GAVE ME A BOOST...

THEN AGAIN, MAYBE THERE'S A BETTER WAY..

SIGH

IF YOU CAN'T CLIMB A TREE, THE OBVIOUS THING TO DO IS TO GET A LADDER..

A STRANGE CREATURE IN WOODSTOCK'S NEST?

MAYBE IT'S A HEDGE TOAD..

THAT'S JUST WHAT I WAS THINKING

I HAVE A BOOK AT HOME THAT TELLS ALL ABOUT SUCH STRANGE CREATURES...I'LL GO GET IT...

HERE IT IS... IT'S CALLED "HEDGE TOADS, QUEEN SNAKES AND GULLY CATS"

I HAVEN'T READ THE BOOK, BUT I READ SOME OF THE REVIEWS

IT LOOKS LIKE WE'RE GOING TO HAVE TO CLIMB THE TREE...

THE ONLY WAY TO FIND OUT WHO'S IN WOODSTOCK'S NEST IS TO CLIMB THIS TREE AND SEE FOR OURSELVES...

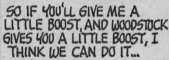

SO IF YOU'LL GIVE ME A LITTLE BOOST, AND WOODSTOCK GIVES YOU A LITTLE BOOST, I THINK WE CAN DO IT...

OKAY... BOOST!

I'M BOOSTING! BUT I'M NOT SURE IF MY BOOSTER IS BOOSTING!

MY DAD TOOK ME TO A BALL GAME YESTERDAY, CHARLIE BROWN..

THEY HAD A REAL DUGOUT, AND A WATER COOLER, AND A BAT RACK AND A DRESSING ROOM.. WE DON'T HAVE ANY OF THOSE THINGS!

DID YOU NOTICE SOMETHING ELSE THAT THEY HAD?

WHAT'S THAT?

REAL PLAYERS!

IN CASE YOU DIDN'T KNOW, THE BALL DOESN'T HAVE TO STOP ROLLING BEFORE YOU CAN PICK IT UP!!

IT WAS HAVING A GOOD TIME, AND I DIDN'T WANT TO DISTURB IT

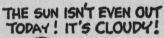

HEY, WHO TOLD YOU THAT YOU COULD PITCH?

YOU PITCH LIKE MY GRANDMOTHER! WHY DON'T YOU GIVE UP? YOU COULDN'T PITCH HAY! WHY DON'T YOU GO BACK WHERE YOU CAME FROM?! BOOOOOOO!!

IT'S HARD WORK BEING BITTER...

THIS HAS BEEN A BAD TIME FOR ME..MAYBE IF I'M LUCKY, TOMORROW WILL BE A BETTER DAY

IN SOME PARTS OF THE WORLD, TOMORROW IS ALREADY TODAY AND TODAY IS YESTERDAY...

IF TOMORROW IS ALREADY TODAY, CHARLIE BROWN, THERE'S NO WAY THAT TOMORROW CAN BE A BETTER DAY

YOU'RE A LOT OF FUN TO HAVE AROUND

I SAW A MOVIE RECENTLY ABOUT A BOY AND HIS DOG

THEY WERE STANDING BY A LAKE AS WE ARE, AND THE BOY PICKED UP A STICK AND THREW IT INTO THE WATER AND THE DOG SWAM OUT AFTER IT AND BROUGHT IT BACK..

➤

RATS! I NEVER FIND ANY ARROWHEADS!

I TALKED WITH MY OPHTHALMOLOGIST TODAY

SO?

HE SAID THAT ALL HUMAN EYES ARE VERY CLOSE TO TWENTY-FIVE MILLIMETERS IN DIAMETER..HE SAID THAT SOME PEOPLE'S EYES APPEAR LARGER BECAUSE OF A WIDE LID FISSURE

THEREFORE, IT IS NOT TRUE THAT PEOPLE WITH LARGE EYES NEED MORE SLEEP THAN PEOPLE WITH SMALL EYES...

I KNOW A KID IN SCHOOL WHO BELONGS TO FOUR BOOK CLUBS!

I THINK IT WAS ONE OF THE BEST MOVIES I'VE EVER SEEN...

I KNEW YOU'D LIKE IT

SIP!

AFTERWARD, WE WENT TO THIS ART GALLERY, AND SAW ALL OF THESE WILD NEW PAINTINGS...

SOME OF THEM, OF COURSE, WERE QUITE HUGE...

THERE WAS ONE THAT WAS ALL DIFFERENT SHADES OF RED..

SIP!

→

"I love you, too," he answered.

"My love for you is higher than the highest mountain which is Mount Everest which is over twenty-nine thousand feet high."

"My love for you is deeper than the deepest ocean which is the Marianas trench which is over thirty-five thousand feet deep."

MY HERO IS A TERRIBLE BORE!

THAT WAS A GOOD DIVE..

HAD IT BEEN INTO MY WATER DISH, I WOULD EVEN CALL IT A BEAUTIFUL DIVE...HOWEVER, IT WAS NOT INTO MY WATER DISH... IT WAS INTO MY SUPPER DISH!

YOU STUPID KID, WHO LIVES CLEAR ACROSS ON THE OTHER SIDE OF THE WORLD, SEND BACK MY BEACH BALL!!

WHAT ARE YOU, A COMMUNIST OR SOMETHING?!

SCHOOL STARTS AGAIN NEXT WEEK...

I THINK I'VE RUINED HER EYES FOR GOOD!

⟶

⟹

boot

boot boot boot boot
boot boot boot boot
boot boot boot boot boot

I'M GLAD I CAN'T HEAR WHAT HOWARD COSELL IS SAYING ABOUT THIS...

KLUNK!

THAT'S WHAT IS CALLED
"COMING IN OFF THE BENCH"

BONK!

WOODSTOCK HAS DIFFICULTY RECOVERING FUMBLES...

THAT STUPID WOODSTOCK...
HE LOST HIS BOOK WITH
ALL OUR SECRET PLAYS!

TWENTY THOUSAND LAPS
AROUND THE FIELD!

IF YOU DON'T PLAY EVERY DAY, YOU LOSE THAT FINE EDGE...

THE WONDERFUL WORLD OF PEANUTS

☐ 12544 6 What Next, Charlie Brown (26)   60p
☐ 15135 8 You're the Greatest, Charlie Brown (27)   60p
☐ 15829 8 It's For You Snoopy (28)   50p
☐ 15828 X Have It Your Way, Charlie Brown (29)   50p
☐ 15698 8 You're Not For Real Snoopy (30)   50p
☐ 15696 1 You're a Pal, Snoopy (31)   60p
☐ 16712 2 What Now Charlie Brown (32)   50p
☐ 17322 X You're Something Special Snoopy (33)   50p
☐ 17417 X You've Got A Friend,
             Charlie Brown (34)   50p
☐ 17844 2 Take It Easy, Charlie Brown (35)   50p
☐ 17861 2 Who Was That Dog I Saw You With,
             Charlie Brown? (36)   50p
☐ 18303 9 There's No-one like you Snoopy (37)   60p
☐ 18663 1 Your Choice Snoopy (38)   50p
☐ 18831 6 Try It Again Charlie Brown (39)   50p
☐ 19550 9 You've Got It Made Snoopy (40)   50p
☐ 19858 3 Don't Give Up Charlie Brown (41)   50p
☐ 19927 X You're So Smart Snoopy (42)   60p
☐ 20491 5 You're On Your Own Snoopy (43)   60p
☐ 20754 X You Can't Win Them All
             Charlie Brown (44)   50p
☐ 21236 5 It's All Yours Snoopy (45)   50p
☐ 21797 9 Watch Out Charlie Brown (46)   50p
☐ 21983 1 You've Got To Be You, Snoopy (47)   50p
☐ 22159 3 You've Come a Long Way, Snoopy (48)   60p
☐ 22304 9 That's Life Snoopy (49)   50p
☐ 22778 8 It's Your Turn Snoopy (50)   50p

Numbers 1-25 and all the above Peanuts titles are available at your local bookshop or newsagent, or can be ordered direct from the publisher. Just tick the titles you want and fill in the form below.
Prices and availability subject to change without notice.

CORONET BOOKS, P.O. Box 11, Falmouth, Cornwall.
Please send cheque or postal order, and allow the following for postage and packing:
U.K.—One book 22p plus 10p per copy for each additional book ordered, up to a maximum of 82p.
B.F.P.O. and EIRE—22p for the first book plus 10p per copy for the next 6 books, thereafter 4p per book.

OTHER OVERSEAS CUSTOMERS—30p for the first book and 10p per copy for each additional book.

Name ....

Address ....

....